Ministry Organizer

Name: ______________________________

Address: ______________________________

City/State/Zip: ______________________________

Phone: ______________________________

Email: ______________________________

Congregation: ______________________________

Congregation Address: ______________________________

Congregation Phone: ______________________________

www.MinistryOrganizer.com

ISBN#: 978-1-941775-35-6

January	February	March	April	May	June
1	1	1	1	1	1
2	2	2	2	2	2
3	3	3	3	3	3
4	4	4	4	4	4
5	5	5	5	5	5
6	6	6	6	6	6
7	7	7	7	7	7
8	8	8	8	8	8
9	9	9	9	9	9
10	10	10	10	10	10
11	11	11	11	11	11
12	12	12	12	12	12
13	13	13	13	13	13
14	14	14	14	14	14
15	15	15	15	15	15
16	16	16	16	16	16
17	17	17	17	17	17
18	18	18	18	18	18
19	19	19	19	19	19
20	20	20	20	20	20
21	21	21	21	21	21
22	22	22	22	22	22
23	23	23	23	23	23
24	24	24	24	24	24
25	25	25	25	25	25
26	26	26	26	26	26
27	27	27	27	27	27
28	28	28	28	28	28
29	29	29	29	29	29
30		30	30	30	30
31		31	31	31	31

July	August	September	October	November	December
1	1	1	1	1	1
2	2	2	2	2	2
3	3	3	3	3	3
4	4	4	4	4	4
5	5	5	5	5	5
6	6	6	6	6	6
7	7	7	7	7	7
8	8	8	8	8	8
9	9	9	9	9	9
10	10	10	10	10	10
11	11	11	11	11	11
12	12	12	12	12	12
13	13	13	13	13	13
14	14	14	14	14	14
15	15	15	15	15	15
16	16	16	16	16	16
17	17	17	17	17	17
18	18	18	18	18	18
19	19	19	19	19	19
20	20	20	20	20	20
21	21	21	21	21	21
22	22	22	22	22	22
23	23	23	23	23	23
24	24	24	24	24	24
25	25	25	25	25	25
26	26	26	26	26	26
27	27	27	27	27	27
28	28	28	28	28	28
29	29	29	29	29	29
30	30	30	30	30	30
31	31	31	31	31	31

January	February	March
April	**May**	**June**

July	August	September

October	November	December

Awesome People

Month

	Hours	Magazines	Tracts	Books	RV	Studies
1						
2						
3						
4						
5						
6						
7						
8						
9						
10						
11						
12						
13						
14						
15						
16						

	Hours	Magazines	Tracts	Books	RV	Studies
17						
18						
19						
20						
21						
22						
23						
24						
25						
26						
27						
28						
29						
30						
31						
	total	total	total	total	total	total

Month

Monday	Tuesday	Wednesday

Thursday	Friday	Saturday/Sunday	

Month

	Hours	Magazines	Tracts	Books	RV	Studies
1						
2						
3						
4						
5						
6						
7						
8						
9						
10						
11						
12						
13						
14						
15						
16						

	Hours	Magazines	Tracts	Books	RV	Studies
17						
18						
19						
20						
21						
22						
23						
24						
25						
26						
27						
28						
29						
30						
31						
	total	total	total	total	total	total

Month

Monday	Tuesday	Wednesday

Thursday	Friday	Saturday/Sunday	

Month

	Hours	Magazines	Tracts	Books	RV	Studies
1						
2						
3						
4						
5						
6						
7						
8						
9						
10						
11						
12						
13						
14						
15						
16						

	Hours	Magazines	Tracts	Books	RV	Studies
17						
18						
19						
20						
21						
22						
23						
24						
25						
26						
27						
28						
29						
30						
31						
	total	total	total	total	total	total

Month

Monday	Tuesday	Wednesday

Thursday	Friday	Saturday/Sunday	

Month

	Hours	Magazines	Tracts	Books	RV	Studies
1						
2						
3						
4						
5						
6						
7						
8						
9						
10						
11						
12						
13						
14						
15						
16						

	Hours	Magazines	Tracts	Books	RV	Studies
17						
18						
19						
20						
21						
22						
23						
24						
25						
26						
27						
28						
29						
30						
31						
	total	total	total	total	total	total

Month

Monday	Tuesday	Wednesday

Thursday	Friday	Saturday/Sunday	

Month

	Hours	Magazines	Tracts	Books	RV	Studies
1						
2						
3						
4						
5						
6						
7						
8						
9						
10						
11						
12						
13						
14						
15						
16						

	Hours	Magazines	Tracts	Books	RV	Studies
17						
18						
19						
20						
21						
22						
23						
24						
25						
26						
27						
28						
29						
30						
31						
	total	total	total	total	total	total

Month

Monday	Tuesday	Wednesday

Thursday	Friday	Saturday/Sunday	

Month

	Hours	Magazines	Tracts	Books	RV	Studies
1						
2						
3						
4						
5						
6						
7						
8						
9						
10						
11						
12						
13						
14						
15						
16						

	Hours	Magazines	Tracts	Books	RV	Studies
17						
18						
19						
20						
21						
22						
23						
24						
25						
26						
27						
28						
29						
30						
31						
	total	total	total	total	total	total

Month

Monday	Tuesday	Wednesday

Thursday	Friday	Saturday/Sunday	

Month

	Hours	Magazines	Tracts	Books	RV	Studies
1						
2						
3						
4						
5						
6						
7						
8						
9						
10						
11						
12						
13						
14						
15						
16						

	Hours	Magazines	Tracts	Books	RV	Studies
17						
18						
19						
20						
21						
22						
23						
24						
25						
26						
27						
28						
29						
30						
31						
	total	total	total	total	total	total

Month

Monday	Tuesday	Wednesday

Thursday	Friday	Saturday/Sunday	

Month

	Hours	Magazines	Tracts	Books	RV	Studies
1						
2						
3						
4						
5						
6						
7						
8						
9						
10						
11						
12						
13						
14						
15						
16						

	Hours	Magazines	Tracts	Books	RV	Studies
17						
18						
19						
20						
21						
22						
23						
24						
25						
26						
27						
28						
29						
30						
31						
	total	total	total	total	total	total

Month

Monday	Tuesday	Wednesday

Thursday	Friday	Saturday/Sunday	

Month

	Hours	Magazines	Tracts	Books	RV	Studies
1						
2						
3						
4						
5						
6						
7						
8						
9						
10						
11						
12						
13						
14						
15						
16						

	Hours	Magazines	Tracts	Books	RV	Studies
17						
18						
19						
20						
21						
22						
23						
24						
25						
26						
27						
28						
29						
30						
31						
	total	total	total	total	total	total

Month

Monday	Tuesday	Wednesday

Thursday	Friday	Saturday/Sunday	

Month

	Hours	Magazines	Tracts	Books	RV	Studies
1						
2						
3						
4						
5						
6						
7						
8						
9						
10						
11						
12						
13						
14						
15						
16						

	Hours	Magazines	Tracts	Books	RV	Studies
17						
18						
19						
20						
21						
22						
23						
24						
25						
26						
27						
28						
29						
30						
31						
	total	total	total	total	total	total

Month

Monday	Tuesday	Wednesday

Thursday	Friday	Saturday/Sunday	

Month

	Hours	Magazines	Tracts	Books	RV	Studies
1						
2						
3						
4						
5						
6						
7						
8						
9						
10						
11						
12						
13						
14						
15						
16						

	Hours	Magazines	Tracts	Books	RV	Studies
17						
18						
19						
20						
21						
22						
23						
24						
25						
26						
27						
28						
29						
30						
31						
	total	total	total	total	total	total

Month

Monday	Tuesday	Wednesday

Thursday	Friday	Saturday/Sunday	

Month

	Hours	Magazines	Tracts	Books	RV	Studies
1						
2						
3						
4						
5						
6						
7						
8						
9						
10						
11						
12						
13						
14						
15						
16						

	Hours	Magazines	Tracts	Books	RV	Studies
17						
18						
19						
20						
21						
22						
23						
24						
25						
26						
27						
28						
29						
30						
31						
	total	total	total	total	total	total

Month

Monday	Tuesday	Wednesday

Thursday	Friday	Saturday/Sunday	

www.ingramcontent.com/pod-product-compliance
Lightning Source LLC
Chambersburg PA
CBHW052034030426
42337CB00027B/4997
* 9 7 8 1 9 4 1 7 7 5 3 5 6 *